Grace Darling Workbook

By Sarah Lee

Grace Darling Workbook© 2014 by Sarah Lee

Contents

Longstone Lighthouse

Sketch the picture of Longstone Lighthouse below.

Grace Darling Haiku

Many poems were written about Grace Darling. Including Haiku poems like this one.

Enormous the waves,
Dark, cold, wet stormy weather,
Grace gripped on the oars.

Fighting the strong tide
With her father by her side
She saved those nine lives.

Grace Darling so young,
Strong, Courageous heroine,
We remember her.

Haiku poems have three lines.
- Line 1 has 5 syllables.
- Line 2 has 7 syllables
- Line 3 has 5 syllables.
- Now try writing your own Haiku poem about Grace Darling and the stormy sea.

_____

_____

_____

_____

_____

_____

_____

_____

_____

_____

_____

_____

Fill in the Missing Words

Fill in the missing words.

Grace Darling lived in a ....

Grace and her father rowed in the stormy ....

They found ....people clinging to the rocks.

The wreck had split in ....

They took the .... back to the lighthouse.

Grace was given gold and silver .... for her bravery.

    people   two   nine   lighthouse   sea   medals

The Story of Grace Darling

Grace Darling, lighthouse, cobble, boat, row, sailors, rocks, storm, Forfarshire, father, mother, nine, people, rescued.

Using the picture and the words above for ideas, write your own story about Grace Darling and the rescue.

_____
_____
_____
_____
_____
_____
_____
_____
_____
_____
_____
_____
_____
_____

Grace Darling Play

Act one can be used as a drama lesson using three characters, Grace, her mother and father using a telescope for a prop. Sound effects using thunder and howling wind would help to make it more dramatic. Practice in threes and perform your act to an audience then plan Act Two and how you would write it.

Characters:

Grace Darling
Mr Darling
Mrs Darling

Act One.

Night time, inside Longstone Lighthouse, the weather is stormy outside, the wind is howling.
Grace is in bed sleeping, Mr Darling is standing over her.

MR DARLING	Grace, Grace, sorry to wake you honey, it's four am, and I am going to bed for a few hours will you take over from me for a while?
GRACE	Of course Father, you get some rest.
MR DARLING	Thanks honey, wake me around seven.
GRACE	Okay Father, see you later.

Mr Darling leaves the room. Grace rubs her eyes and gets out of bed and gets dressed quickly, then climbs the stairs to the lamp. She checks the lamp is working, the oil is topped up. Then looks outside. Thunder is heard. Lightning flashes. She picks up her telescope and looks outside.

GRACE	Oh No! Look at the size of those waves! It's so stormy out there.

Grace continues to look outside; the thunder and howling wind get louder. She thinks she has spotted something. She stares through her telescope.

GRACE	No it can't be!

Grace opens the door to the balcony, and steps outside into the stormy rainy night. She steadies herself holding the railing and stares through her telescope. Then she hurries downstairs to wake her father and mother.

GRACE	Father, wake up, come quickly.
MR DARLING	What is it?
GRACE	Father there is a ship against the rocks.
MR DARLING	Okay I'm coming.

Grace goes back to the lantern followed by her father and mother. They all take turns to look through the telescope.

MR DARLING	You are right, it looks like it is wrecked, it looks in a bad way, and there may not even be any survivors. The weather is atrocious. Look at the size of those waves.
GRACE	Father, we need to go out to see, there may be survivors.
MR DARLING	It is too dangerous to go in our small boat in this weather Grace. If the sea can do that much damage to a big ship like that, what could it do to our little rowing boat? There may not even be any survivors.

Grace looks again out to the wreck. She spots something.

GRACE	Father! Look! There are some people clinging to the rock.

Mr Darling takes the telescope and looks at the wreck.

MR DARLING	You are right there are some people on the rock. But it is far too dangerous to rescue them, we will wait for the storm to calm down.

GRACE	But Father, they may die because of the cold, or they may get swept out to sea, we need to go now father. It is almost light now, we can see better.
MRS DARLING	No! It is far too dangerous; I could lose a husband and a daughter. No, you should wait until the storm dies down, your father is right.
GRACE	They are in need Father, their lives depend on us, God will protect us, please Father, I cannot stand by and watch them die.
MR DARLING	Okay, let's get the cobble out. Wrap up warm, put on your hat and tie it tight.

Grace hugs her father. Her mother starts crying. Grace hugs her mother.

Using lined paper with a wide margin, or you can type it using the computer, write the script for Act Two. Remember to put in the character's names in the margin and there is no need to use speech marks in a script. Don't forget your setting descriptions.

Daily News

7th September 1838

Mighty Storm Wrecks Ship 43 Dead

Last night the new paddle steamer the Forfarshire left Hull harbour in calm waters and with 61 people on board, including the crew and passengers, headed for Dundee. A mighty storm began around 11 pm with 90 mph gales. The Paddle steamer, struggling against the power of the waves, lost engine power as their pumps began leaking. The ship was at the mercy of the wind and waves and drifted towards the Farne Islands and struck Big Harker Rock around 3am. The waves were so high, they picked up the ship and threw it against the rocks breaking it in two halves. Many lives were lost immediately. A

crew of eight men and one passenger were picked up in a lifeboat twenty miles from the wreck. Nine other survivors were rescued from the rock by the lighthouse keeper of Longstone lighthouse and his daughter twenty two year old Grace Darling. A rescue boat from

North Sunderland also put out to sea to aid the passengers, but they too now are stranded at Longstone Lighthouse. Weather experts say the storm will last for another two days.

More to follow.

Daily News

7th September 1838

Write your own news story about the ship wreck.

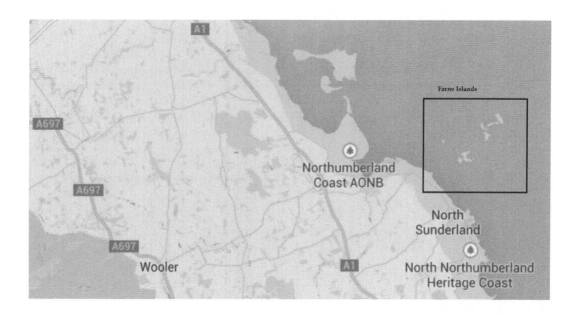

On the map below, The Farne Islands cannot be seen.
Draw a square on the map where the Farne Islands are and label
it.

Label the Farne Islands

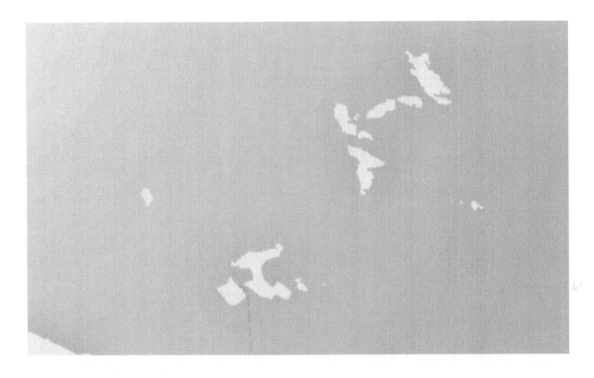

1. Colour in the map and make a key to show these places:
Longstone Island, Big Harker, Brownsman Island, Inner Farne,
Stapleton Island. .

☐

☐

☐

☐

☐

Using Co-ordinates

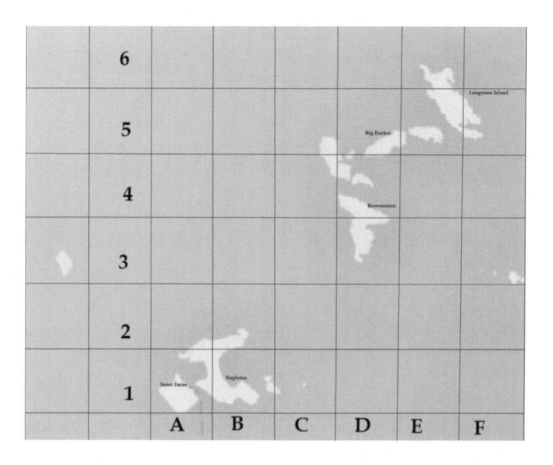

Look at the map above. The co-ordinates for Stapleton Island are A1, A2, B1 and B2.

What are the co-ordinates for:

1. Longstone Island?

2. Inner Farne?

3. Big Harker?

4. Brownsman Island?

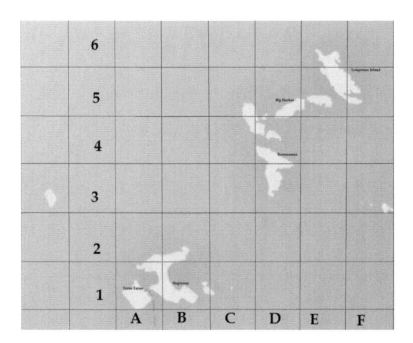

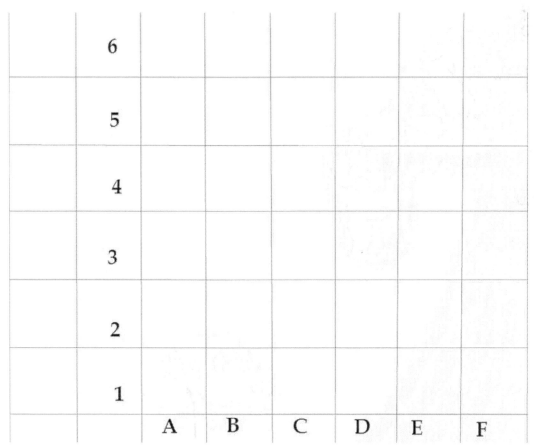

Copy the Farne Islands onto the map above.

Design a New Island for Grace Darling

Grace Darling lived on a barren Island. The only two buildings were the lighthouse and the barracks.

Map data ©2014 Google

Using the map above draw how you would change the Island if you had the resources. Think about paths, recreation, buildings etc.

Comprehension

Read the text below from "The Diary of Grace Darling' by Sarah Lee.

I pulled on the oar with both hands, but the water felt like it wanted to rip it away from me. My skin was wet and cold, and every piece of clothing was soaked through. A wave broke near the boat, and the spray burst upon me, soaking me again and taking my breath away. Father too was soaked, water dripped from his coat, but he never stopped rowing and urged me to do the same. I worried in case I didn't have enough strength, and would cause him suffering having to row harder to compensate for my weakness. I pulled on the oar in rhythm to Father's pull, and tried to pull as hard. I prayed to God as I rowed that the people would be saved and our lives to be spared. We were at God's mercy in a small boat in the fury of the wild ocean and mighty wind. I worried in case we were too late and find only the bodies of those poor souls if they had not been swept out to sea.

We we rewarded with the sound of cries for help, as we neared Harkers Rock, my heart leaped with delight knowing there were still some people alive. It gave me energy and we found the strength to row faster towards them. As we neared the wreck I could see the horror before me. Several bodies were floating in the sea around us. The look on their faces were looks I shall never forget. Some people were still clinging to the wreck, some were on the rocks, there were nine people that I could see. As we got closer the people started gathering on the edge of the rock. Some were laughing and singing praises to God, some were crying, a woman was howling. They looked like they were all going to leap into the boat at once. I worried because this would surely capsize the boat and all our lives would be lost.

What almost ripped away from her?...

Describe some of the worries Grace had as she neared the wreck?

....

....

....

....

....

....

....

....

Why did her heart leap with delight?

....
....
....
....

How do we know from the text that Grace believed in God?

....
....
....
....
....
....
....
....

Describe the scene she saw as she neared the wreck.

....
....
....
....
....
....
....
....
....

Describe a time you can remember when you have felt nervous or afraid.

....

....

....

....

....

Why was Grace Darling viewed as a heroine?

....

....

....

....

....

....

....

Religious Inspiration

Explain how Grace's belief in God influenced her actions on the day she rescued those people from the rock.

_____

_____

_____

_____

_____

_____

_____

_____

_____

_____

_____

_____

_____

_____

_____

_____

_____

_____

Design a Victorian Costume

In 'The Diary of Grace Darling' are some wedding dress designs.

Design a Victorian dress for Grace.

Grace Darling Wordsearch

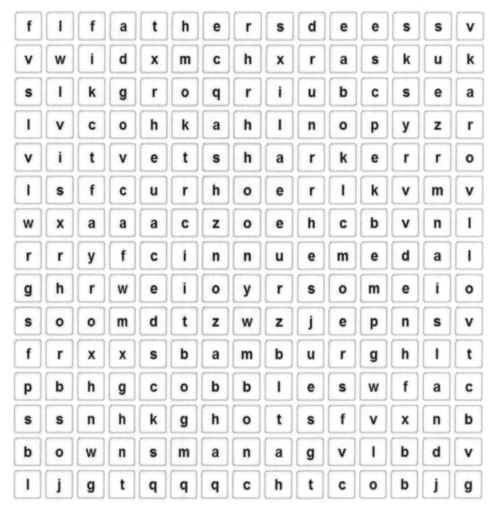

f	l	f	a	t	h	e	r	s	d	e	e	s	s	v
v	w	i	d	x	m	c	h	x	r	a	s	k	u	k
s	l	k	g	r	o	q	r	i	u	b	c	s	e	a
l	v	c	o	h	k	a	h	l	n	o	p	y	z	r
v	i	t	v	e	t	s	h	a	r	k	e	r	r	o
l	s	f	c	u	r	h	o	e	r	l	k	v	m	v
w	x	a	a	a	c	z	o	e	h	c	b	v	n	l
r	r	y	f	c	i	n	n	u	e	m	e	d	a	l
g	h	r	w	e	i	o	y	r	s	o	m	e	i	o
s	o	o	m	d	t	z	w	z	j	e	p	n	s	v
f	r	x	x	s	b	a	m	b	u	r	g	h	l	t
p	b	h	g	c	o	b	b	l	e	s	w	f	a	c
s	s	n	h	k	g	h	o	t	s	f	v	x	n	b
b	o	w	n	s	m	a	n	a	g	v	l	b	d	v
l	j	g	t	q	q	q	c	h	t	c	o	b	j	g

Find the following words in the wordsearch.

grace	longstone	island	
lighthouse	cobble	wreck	
forfarshire	sea	storm	father
row	rocks	harker	bamburgh
medal	boat		

Portrait Art

Grace had many artists painting her portrait.
Copy the portrait in the box below.

Draw Your Own Portrait

Wildlife of the Farne Islands

The Puffin

The puffins breed on the rocky cliffs and shores of the Farne Islands. They develop a brightly coloured beak in the breeding season giving them an appearance similar to a parrot, and are often called sea parrots. The coloured parts drop off after the breeding season leaving a duller beak. They feed by diving under the water and feed on sand eels, herring and capelin. They emigrate in the autumn and return in the spring. Millions of the Atlanic Puffins spend the winter in Iceland. Puffins dig burrows to lay their egg, and laying only one egg often lay their egg in a rabbit burrow.

Why are puffins often called sea parrots?

....

....

What do puffins feed on?

....

....

Where to the puffins migrate to in the autumn?

....

....

How many eggs do puffins lay at one time?

....

Draw a Puffin

Copy the Puffin

The Seal

Thousands of seals live on the Farne Islands. They are often called pinnipeds, and are slender barrel shaped mammals. Their bodies suit them well for diving, and are experts and can stay under water for over an hour. They communicate with each other by beating their fins on the water and grunting or barking. They feed on squid, shellfish, fish and small marine animals. They are hunted by sharks and Orcas. Although it is rare to find sharks in the waters near the Farne Islands, Orcas, known as killer whales, swim in these waters.

What is the other name for seal?

....

How do they communicate with each other?

....

....

....

What do the seals feed on?

....

....

Which animals hunt seals?

....

....

The Eider Duck

Eider ducks are the largest ducks in the UK. They live around the northern coasts in the UK including The Farne Islands. They eat mollusks such as mussels and crustaceans such as crabs. The male bird, the drake, is black and white and has pale green cheeks, and a grey beak. The female bird is brown with black spotted feathers and has a grey beak. They like to make their nests on Islands and they lay around 3 to 5 eggs at one time. Eider ducks are sometimes called Cuddy's ducks, as St Cuthbert back in the 7th century, grew fond of them as they lived on his Island, Inner Farne, and helped to make laws to protect them.

Describe the male Eider duck.

....

....

....

What do Eider ducks eat?

....

....

....

How many eggs do they lay at one time?

....

What is the other name for Eider ducks?

....

Draw an Eider Duck

Make a Gingerbread Lighthouse

Ingredients

- 375g of plain flour
- 125g butter at room temperature
- 125 mls of golden syrup
- 100g of brown sugar
- 1 egg
- 1 tablespoon ground ginger
- 1 teaspoon of bicarbonate of soda
- Plain flour to dust.
- Ready made icing

Method

1. Beat butter and sugar together in a bowl until creamy with a whisk or wooden spoon.
2. Separate egg from yolk, add yoke to mixture.
3. Add golden syrup and beat until creamy.
4. Stir in flour, ground ginger and bicarbonate of soda.
5. Mix together and knead on floured surface.
6. Put mixture in the fridge for 30 minutes.

7. Heat oven to 180 degrees C

8. After the thirty minutes place dough between two sheets of baking paper and roll out until it is about 1cm thick.

9. Carefully cut out lighthouse shapes from dough and place on oiled tray so they are 3cm apart.

10. Bake in the oven for around 10 minutes or until brown.

11. Remove from oven and cool on wire rack.

12. Decorate with ready made icing.

Grace Darling in Victorian Times

Look carefully at the picture on the previous page. This is what Grace Darling's desk may have looked like as she lived in Victorian times. .

Make a list of all the items on the desk.

_____

_____

_____

_____

_____

_____

_____

_____

How different would her desk look today?_____

_____

_____

_____

_____

_____

_____

_____

_____

_____

Draw a picture of the items on Grace Darling's desk in how it would look today.

Sorting Victorian and Modern Items

Cut out the pictures and match them. Then sort them into Victorian items and items today and stick them on table on following page. .

Victorian Times   Today

Make a Lighthouse Pencil Holder

You can make a model of a lighthouse using paper, clay or play dough, papier mache or plaster of paris bandage like was used in the picture above.

To make the model above you will need:
- Two cylinder shaped boxes such as a Jaffa cake tube and gravy tub.
- A plastic cup
- Scissors
- Sellotape
- Plaster of paris bandages (400g or 3 bandages- less if using smaller cylinders)
- Dish of water

1. Cut the smaller cylinder box in half.
2. Stand the taller cylinder box inside one of the halves but secure the bottom with sellotape or blu tack so it doesn't wobble about. Sellotape the two halves of the small cylinder box together side by side.

3. Place the cup on top of the tall cylinder; you may have to cut off the rim of the cup to make it fit.
4. Cut off some of the plaster of paris bandage and dip it in the dish of water for a few seconds. Squeeze out some of the excess water, then carefully wrap the wet bandage around the tall tower, overlapping if need be.
5. Continue to cover the whole model in the wet bandage. It may need two or three layers.
6. Smooth it out with your fingers whilst it is still wet.
7. Leave it to dry overnight at least.
8. Paint model.
9. Make a rim for your lighthouse by cutting out a hollow circle from card. The inside circle should be as wide as the rim of the cup so it will slide over the top. Or you could cut a strip and glue it around.

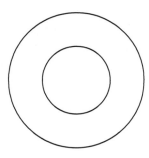

10.   Make a top for your lighthouse by cutting a circle out of card.

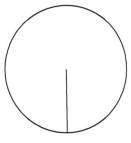

11.   Cut a slit to the centre, then fold it into a cone shape and sellotape it to fit the top of the tower. Glue in place.

Paper Lighthouse Model

Equipment.

Paper cut out model on page following page. .

Glue stick.

Scissors.

Pencil and colouring pencils.

Cut out model carefully from following page cutting around tabs. Decorate model, drawing in windows etc. Fold four sections along lines. Fold tabs to make a crease. Use a glue stick and paste glue on tabs on side and on roof. Fold model holding side of model for a few seconds until glued tab holds firm. Gently press roof together and holding for a few seconds while glue holds.

You could make a model Island and glue the lighthouse to the Island.

If you want to glue model to a base, glue tabs on bottom and press to base. If you don't want a base then just cut bottom tabs off.

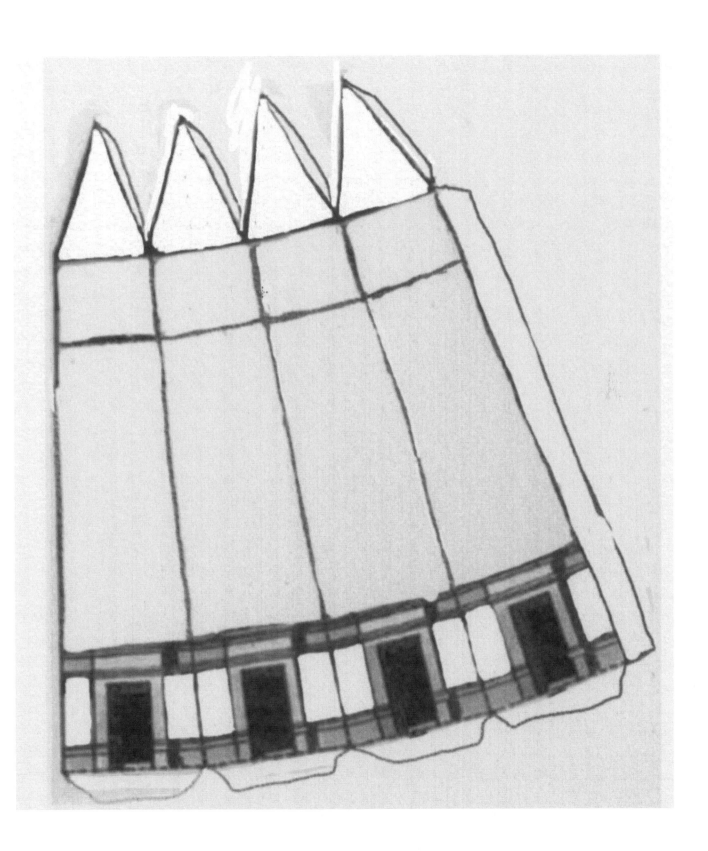

Other Books by Sarah Lee

All available on Amazon.

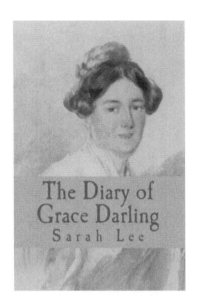

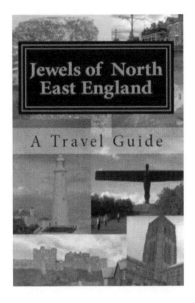

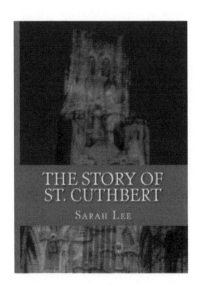

Notes